FOREWORD

THIS is a book for beginners. Its aim is (a) to provide plenty of easy material, suitably graded, since confidence and fluency in sight-singing can only be developed by success, and (b) to teach by practice the small amount of basic knowledge necessary for reading music.

The ability to sing, stepwise, up and down the tonic-sol-fa scale is almost a pre-requisite. Where it is not present it should be acquired right at the start, the earliest exercises being sung first from a simple modulator and then from a large stave on the blackboard. The singers should always point at the notes as they sing them, and sing first to the tonic-sol-fa syllables and afterwards to vocalised sounds and even to words if the teacher (or class) cares to provide them.

Ultimately indeed, singers should be able to read words and music simultaneously, but it must be emphasised that this is an elementary book, and one which it is hoped the class will be able to manage right to the end. So often as sight-singing books get harder, the class ceases to be able to "read" the exercises and either the book is abandoned or else the class laboriously "learns" the exercises, which is a waste of time.

After the earliest exercises the material is largely the simple hymn tune (in ordinary time values) or folk tune. Plenty of further material can therefore be found in the hymn-book and song-book, but it must be chosen carefully. *The Folk Song Sight Singing Series* (O.U.P.) has been freely drawn upon, but with a different principle of grading from that followed there. Here stepwise practice and the open key come first. The scheme of this book had its origins in *Eyes Right* by Cyril Winn, to whom grateful acknowledgement is made.

The number of exercises attempted in any lesson must be governed by the ability of the class. Sight-singing should obviously occupy no more than part of a singing lesson and when that time has been spent it is unwise to continue in the hope of "getting on". However much or little has been achieved in that time, the class should always be left with a feeling of confidence. To this end it is often a sound principle to include some earlier easier exercises as revision.

To help in finding *doh* it is as well to point out very frequently that the last sharp in the key signature is *te* and the last flat *fah*, but it is not enough merely to remind the class of this principle—it must constantly be practised if recognition is to be instantaneous.

R. W. A.

SING AT SIGHT

by

WILLIAM APPLEBY

Learn: When there are no SHARPS (♯) or FLATS (♭) **DOH** is either 𝄞 or 𝄞

Learn: When the bottom figure of the time signature is 4 (as here ♩) ♩ (CROTCHET) is one beat long.

Learn: When the notes go **UP**, you go **UP**, and when the notes go **DOWN**, you go **DOWN**.

Sing:

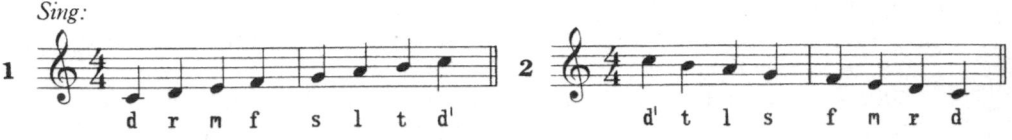

Learn: When ♩ (crotchet) is one beat long, ♩ (MINIM) is two beats long.

Sing:

Learn: When ♩ (crotchet) = 1, 𝄽 (crotchet rest) = 1 beat rest.

Sing:

Learn: When the notes stay still, *you* stay still.
   Sing:

Learn: When there is one sharp (♯) doh is [music] or [music]
   Sing:

Sing at Sight

4

Learn: When there is one flat (♭) doh is either or

Sing at Sight

Learn: A DOT after a note makes it half as long again. Thus if ♩(minim) = 2, then ♩·(dotted minim) = 3.

Sing:

Learn: Passages between dots (like the four bars below) must be repeated. *D.C. al Fine* means go back to the beginning and continue to the word *FINE* (finish).

Try to sing the PHRASES (marked ⌒) in one breath.

8

German

66

FINE

D.C. al Fine

Russian

67

Flemish

68

German

69

German (adapted)

70

Learn: When ♩ (crotchet) = 1, ○ (SEMIBREVE) = 4.

Learn:

d m s m   d m s m   f l d¹ l   f l d¹ l   s t r¹t   s t r¹t   d¹s m s   d

Learn: When there are two sharps, doh is either or

Learn:

d m s m   d m s m   f l d¹ l   f l d¹ l   s t r¹t   s t r¹t   d¹s m s   d

Sing at Sight

Learn: When ♩ (minim) = 2, ♩. (minim rest) is 2 beats rest.

Sing:
German

German

British

Hungarian

German

Tune: Culbach

FINE

D.C. al Fine

British
Sing:

77

76

75

74

73

72

71

Learn: When there are two flats doh is either  or

Learn:

Sing:

German

78

FINE

D.C. al Fine

Learn:
> means accent the note.
⌒ joining the same notes means keep on. This mark is called a TIE.

Sing:

German

79

British

80

Hungarian (adapted)

81

Learn: **C** as a time signature is the same as 4/4

Sing:

Danish

82

Sing at Sight

Piae Cantiones

91

German

92

Learn: When there are three flats doh is either   or   and four sharps   or

Sing: Tune: Benvenuto (Webb) (slightly adapted)

93

German

94

14

Learn: Halve a crotchet (♩) and you get a QUAVER (♪). Quavers are often joined together like this ♫

Sing:

Tune: Dessam (Ahle)

106

Plymouth Collection (U.S.A.) 1855

107

FINE

D.C. al Fine

Learn: The dot and the jerk ♩. ♪

Learn:

1 2 & 1 2 & 1 2 & 1 2

Hold the tied notes

1 2 & 1 2 & 1 2 & 1 2

1 2 & 1 2 & 1 2 & 1 2

Sing:

Welsh

108

British

109

German

110

Sing at Sight

French

111

Tune: Neander

112

Tune: Rodmell

113

Tune: Samson (from Handel)

114

Tune: Mainz

115

Tune: Moscow

116

Source unknown

117

Learn: A sharp in front of a note raises it half a tone like this:

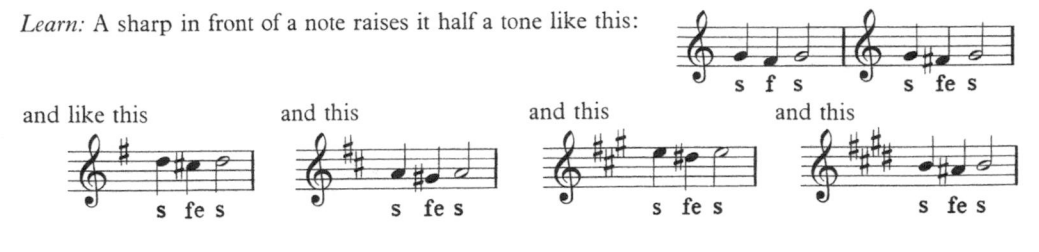

and like this   and this   and this   and this

A NATURAL (♮) when it is in front of a flat note does the same thing.

Sing: Tune: Melcombe *(Webb)*

118

Tune: Llanfair *(R. Williams)*

119

FINE   D. C. al Fine

Tune: York

120

Tune: Capetown

121

Tune: Winchester New

122

Tune: Dundee

123

Sing at Sight

18

Learn: **FE** often follows **ME**

Learn: All the tunes to this point have centred on doh. Most of them have ended on it and many have begun on it. The next group centre on **LAH**, often beginning and ending on it. Tunes centred on doh are called MAJOR tunes; those centred on lah are called MINOR tunes.

We give the tunes names from their central note: a tune centred on C as doh is in C major, but centred on C as lah is C minor.

Some tunes, beginning and ending in the minor, MODULATE (or change) to the major in the middle.

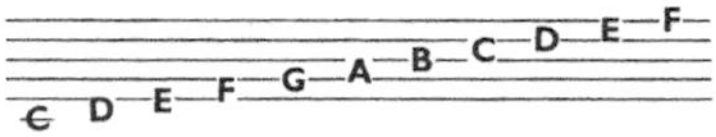

Sing:

Tune: Southwell

129
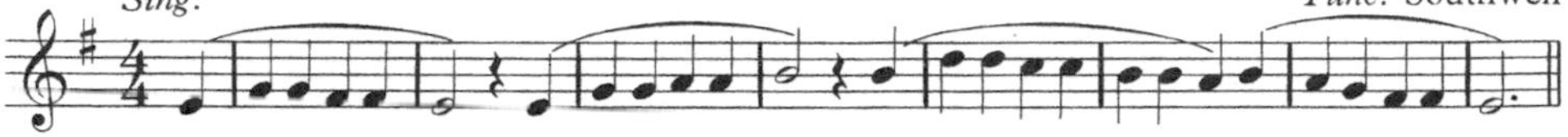

German

130
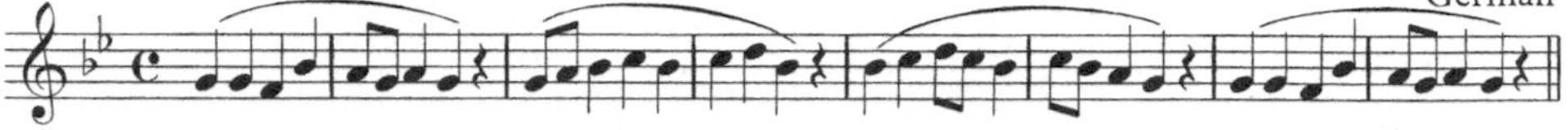

Tune: St. Mary

131
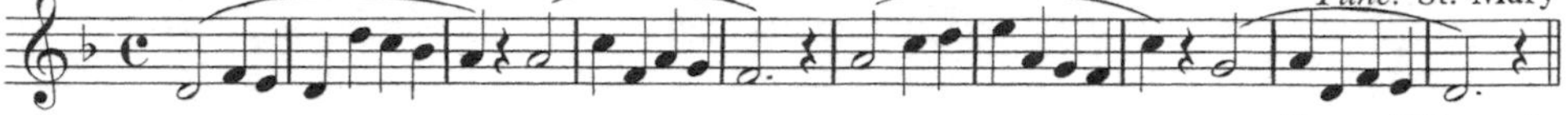

Tune: Old 104th

132
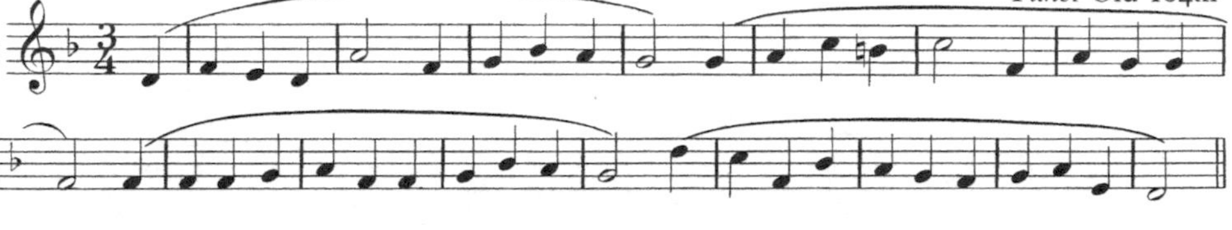

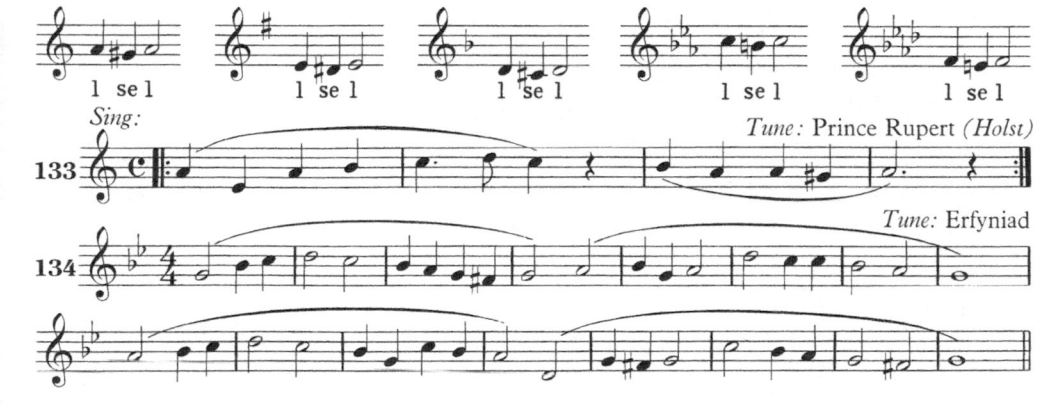

Learn: Very often in minor tunes we come across the note **SE** (pronounced "see" or "zee"). It is half a tone higher than **SOH** and is therefore shewn by a sharp or natural. e.g.

l se l   l se l   l se l   l se l   l se l

Sing:

Tune: Prince Rupert *(Holst)*

133

Tune: Erfyniad

134

Tune: Walsall

135

Basque

136

FINE

D.C. al Fine

Learn: Some tunes begin and end in the major, but modulate to the minor in the middle. This usually involves the note **DE**, half a tone higher than doh.

r de r   r de r   r de r

Sing:

Dutch

137

FINE

D.C. al Fine

Tune: St. Austin

138

It is sometimes easier to change the whole phrase into the minor:

Tune: Abbey

139

r t d f   m r r de r   s
d   t l l   se l

Tune: Bristol

140

r r d f   m r r der   r m
d   t l l   se l

Sing at Sight

Learn: **TE** made half a tone lower becomes **TA**

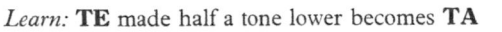

l ta l    l ta l 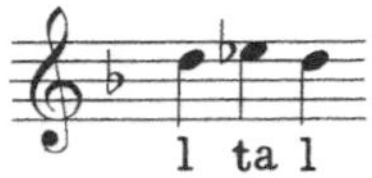   l ta l

Sing: *Tune:* A Virgin most pure

141

Scottish

142

Italian

143

Serbian

144

Tune: Mannheim

145

FINE   *D.C. al Fine*

In all the tunes up to this point, a crotchet has been worth one beat; and the lower figure of the time signature has been **4**.

In the next fifteen tunes, minims and quavers will also be used as units, and their worth one beat. When a minim is worth one beat, the lower figure will be **2**, and when a quaver is worth one beat, the lower figure will be **8**.

You will also meet the quaver rest (⁊) SEMIQUAVERS 𝅘𝅥𝅯𝅘𝅥𝅯 𝅘𝅥𝅯 𝅘𝅥𝅯 and their rests ⁊, the figure 𝅘𝅥𝅭 𝅘𝅥𝅯 and the PAUSE 𝄐

Also *ff f mf mp p pp*   Get louder ⎯⎯ *cresc.* │ get softer ⎯⎯ *dim.* │ get slower *rall.*
LOUD ---------- SOFT

Sing at Sight

Sing:

Tune: Vulpius

When the time signature is $\frac{6}{8}$ try to get the feel of 2 beats (each ♩.) in a bar.

British

British

♩ ♫ get a good jerk and a nice swing

British

French

Sing at Sight

24

Processed and printed by
Halstan & Co. Ltd., Amersham, Bucks., England

OXFORD UNIVERSITY PRESS